Stark County District Library

Magnolia

330.866.

www.starklibrary.org

NOV - - 2007

D1358026

KNOW HOW KNOW WHY

INCREDIBLE INSECTS

Written by Lucy Bater

Illustrations by John Butler

© 2007 Rourke Publishing LLC

All rights reserved. No part of this book may be reproduced or utilized in any form or by any means, electronic or mechanical including photocopying, recording, or by any information storage and retrieval system without permission in writing from the publisher.

www.rourkepublishing.com

Library of Congress Cataloging-in-Publication Data

Bater, Lucy -
    Incredible Insects / Lucy Bater.
            p. cm. -- (Know How, Know Why)
    Includes Bibliographical references and index
    ISBN 1-60044-260-9 (hardcover)
    ISBN 978-1-60044-348-0 (paperback)

Printed in the USA

CG/CG

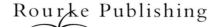

Rourke Publishing

www.rourkepublishing.com – sales@rourkepublishing.com
Post Office Box 3328, Vero Beach, FL 32964

FLYING COLORS

Insects were the first creatures ever to fly. The earliest known fossil insect with wings lived long before dinosaurs—around 350 million years ago! Prehistoric evidence can be found in amber, which is the fossilized resin of pine trees. Attracted by its sweetness, an unsuspecting insect would get stuck and meet a sticky end preserving it for millions of years.

What is an insect

Insects have six legs and their bodies are made of three essential parts—the head, thorax, and abdomen. Most insects also have four wings. Unlike humans, insects have exoskeletons—skeletons on the outside of their bodies. This protects them from harm and ensures that water stays inside preventing their bodies from drying out.

What are arachnids

Arachnids have eight (sometimes ten) legs and they are made of two distinct body parts—the abdomen and the cephalothorax (a combination of the head and thorax). They have a pair of fang-like mouthparts and a pair of leg-like structures that come in useful for holding food. Scorpions, mites, ticks, harvestmen (daddy long-legs), and spiders, are all part of the arachnid family.

FACT BYTES

Stick insects are the longest insects in the world. African stick insects can be as long as 15 3/4 in. (40 cm).

How do insects grow

Growing insects break out of, and shed, their skin, and swell up before the new skin hardens. This process is called "moulting." Once adulthood is reached, they won't get any bigger which is reassuring to know when there are over five million insect species on Earth!

What do insects eat

Insects enjoy a varied menu depending on their species. A tasty insect supper could comprise any of these ingredients: plants, nectar, other insects, blood (if you're a mosquito), and sometimes even the crumbs that drop down near your toe as you read this book and munch your way through that cookie…

Do insects hibernate

Being cold-blooded, insects prefer warmer climes and although they don't exactly hibernate, they do have a clever way of dealing with cold weather. They do this by a process called diapause that makes them stop moving. Some adult insects can stop the water in their bodies from freezing by producing a chemical called glycerol that acts like anti-freeze. Sensibly, honeybees stay in clusters in their hives and use their vibrating wing muscles to raise the temperature and keep warm when it's cold!

Honeybees stay in clusters to keep warm.

FLYING COLORS

WHAT'S BUGGING YOU?

The word "bug" is often used in reference to insects, but bugs are a special group all of their own. They belong to the Hemiptera group, characterized by the sucking mouthparts that come out of the tips of their head. Bugs in this family include bed bugs, assassin bugs, flat bugs, seed bugs, red bugs, stink bugs, plant bugs... got that?

Do bed bugs really bite

A bed bug.

Night night, sleep tight, don't let the bed bugs bite… Just before you close your eyes, the bad news is that, yes, bed bugs really do bite! A female bed bug kept warm and able to access a regular diet of blood can lay up to 200 eggs. Bed bugs hide during the day but beware because they crawl out at night to feast on snoozing humans.

What makes a stink bug stink

A stink bug.

Put yourself in a stink bug's shoes… there's a big bird about to pounce on you and gobble you up, and in a matter of moments you're going to be history—so what would you do? You'd need to unleash hidden powers (or, in this case, pongs) so you can live to see another day. That's exactly what a stink bug does—phew, one whiff of their smelly perfume and predators think twice!

Where does an assassin bug get its name

Lurking in the undergrowth waiting to ambush its prey, an assassin bug lies in wait preparing to assassinate its victim. This bug is a killer insect and eats other bugs by first stabbing them, before injecting a lethal poison into them. If it can't find an insect to eat, rather than go hungry it's quite happy to make do by eating another assassin bug!

An assassin bug.

How do bugs eat

Bugs pierce their food with a long, hollow feeding tube called a proboscis before sucking up all the juices. Some bugs suck plant juices, but there are some more sinister bugs in existence that like to suck blood and body fluids!

Can bugs live under water

Many bugs have adapted to life in, or around, water. Water boatmen look like little boats with legs for oars, which they use to paddle through the water, chasing tadpoles and small fish to eat. Water measurers can be found at the edges of ponds. They "skate" across the water's surface, stabbing at mosquito larvae with their piercing mouthparts. Bugs can even be found in stagnant or polluted water.

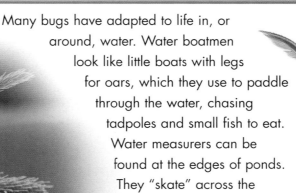

A water boatman.

What is a flying alligator

This is, in fact, called a lantern bug, though you can see why it is known as a flying alligator—it even looks like it has the same eyes, nose and teeth as a real alligator! Its real eyes are on the back of its head, as are its antennae and, of course, it doesn't really have teeth or a nose! It is called a lantern bug because it is supposed to "light up" its head at night, but it doesn't do this either!

FACT BYTES

Ambush bugs use the flowers on which they rest to act as a camouflage before ambushing their prey.

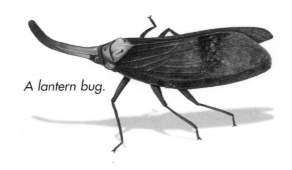

A lantern bug.

BEETLE MANIA

With over 400,000 different kinds, beetles really do rule the insect world! They are the largest group of insects and can be found in all climates. Brightly colored and beautifully patterned, beetles come in black, blue, red, green, and even gold (and the list doesn't stop there).

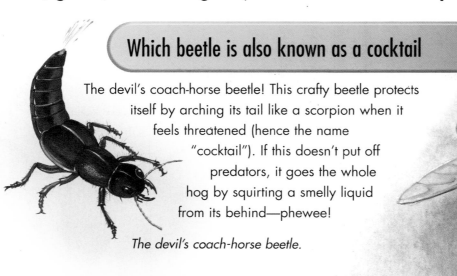

Which beetle is also known as a cocktail ?

The devil's coach-horse beetle! This crafty beetle protects itself by arching its tail like a scorpion when it feels threatened (hence the name "cocktail"). If this doesn't put off predators, it goes the whole hog by squirting a smelly liquid from its behind—phewee!

The devil's coach-horse beetle.

What is a blister beetle ?

These brightly colored beetles are so called because they cause blisters! When handled, they secrete a nasty substance called cantharidin which burns the skin and stings like stinging nettles. They are brightly colored to warn potential predators that they are bad to eat. It's probably best to leave these little beetles well alone!

A blister beetle.

Stag beetles.

Where do baby dung beetles live ?

All that hard work cleaning up the earth and burying dung balls means that female scarab (or dung) beetles are able to lay their eggs in privacy underground—in the dung! As the worm babies hatch they dig into, and live happily inside, the dung ball, before coming up for air as adult dung beetles.

Which beetle looks like a deer

If you've ever seen a male stag beetle flying low on summer evenings you'll know the answer. This mighty beetle, one of the biggest in Europe, can be as big as 2-3 in. (50-70 mm) and has magnificent antler-like jaws. Like deer, these antlers come in very handy when fighting, for male supremacy, over a female.

Which are the largest and smallest beetles

Some large, tropical beetles are as big as human hands, whereas the smallest types can hardly be seen. The largest living insect is the adult goliath beetle. It can measure up to 6 in. (15 cm) long and can weigh up to 3.5 oz (100 g) —that's a heavyweight as big as your fist! Although the rare South American long-horned beetle is thinner, its body length can be over 6 in. (16 cm). Feather-winged beetles are the smallest in the world, measuring only 0.25 mm—watch you don't step on one!

South American long-horned beetle.

Why were scarab beetles worshipped in Egypt

Watching a busy scarab or "dung" beetle at work fascinated ancient Egyptians. As the scarab beetle busily rolled balls of dung along the ground, the scarab's circular shape and bright golden color reminded them of the sun crossing Earth. The scarab symbol was soon used as a good luck charm to ward off evil and symbolize immortality. You've probably come across history book pictures of it on Egyptian tombs and jewelry.

FACT BYTES

The acteon beetle from South America can grow to be a chunky 3 1/2 in. (9 cm) long, 2 in. (5 cm) wide and 1 1/2 in. (4 cm) thick!

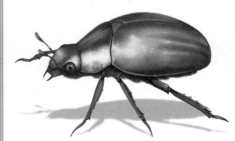

A scarab or "dung" beetle.

EYE SPY DRAGONFLY

There are nearly 2,500 different species of dragonfly—you can watch their metallic green and blue bodies flitting near streams and rivers. Dragonflies existed way before dinosaurs and these ancient insects may have had a wingspan of up to three feet, but disappointingly, modern-day dragonflies are much smaller!

Where did the dragonfly get its name

If you could find a dragonfly dentist they'd soon be able to tell you! A dragonfly has really fierce-looking jaws and belongs to the family called odonata meaning "toothed jaws." Imagine how scary that must look close-up. In the Middle Ages "flies" had a bad name. The term dragonfly probably reflects this negative attitude towards flies.

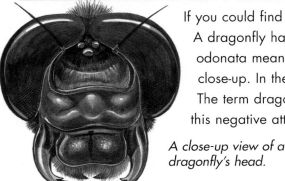

A close-up view of a dragonfly's head.

How do dragonflies kill prey ?

Adult dragonflies catch prey whilst in flight by seizing it with their front legs and chewing it in their powerful jaws. They mainly eat midges and mosquitoes, but will also try butterflies, moths, and even smaller dragonflies. The larvae, which live in water, capture prey using a "mask." Their lower lip is enlarged and has two hooks on it. It is also extendible, so when a larva sees its prey it shoots out its lower lip from the front of its head and pierces the prey item, which is then drawn back to its jaws.

Can they see you coming ?

The answer is simply, yes! Its eyes take up most of its head giving it a 360-degree field of vision. This means it can see in front, above, below and behind, all at the same time—impressive, huh?

Dragonflies return to water to lay eggs.

Why is a dragonfly also called a mosquito hawk

A mosquito.

A typical dragonfly meal consists of any of the following ingredients—mosquitoes, midges, gnats, wasps, and flies. Thanks to its liking for the dreaded mosquito, humans are a big fan of dragonflies, so if you're near a riverbank on a hot summer's day, let's hope the dragonflies are there hunting mosquitoes!

Is a dragonfly a fly

No! Dragonflies are insects with four wings; flies are insects with two wings. Most insects have four wings and flies are actually the exceptions.

Why does a dragonfly have hairy legs

A dragonfly's legs are covered in short bristles. When the dragonfly is out hunting for a tasty snack, its hairy legs

form an oval-shaped basket that scoop its prey right out of the air —just like a shopping basket!

FACT BYTES

The largest dragonfly comes from Central and South America. Its wingspan measures $4^3/4$ in. (12 cm) and its body is $7^1/2$ in. (19 cm) long!

How fast can a dragonfly actually fly

Dragonflies have two pairs of long, thin, membranous wings which they can beat independently. This means that the front wings can be going down while the back ones are coming up. This makes dragonflies excellent fliers. They can loop-the-loop, hover and even fly backwards! These amazing wings mean that most large dragonflies can reach speeds of about 18 mph (30 km/h), but the Australian dragonfly, *Austrophlebia costalis*, beats them all. It has been recorded doing 36 mph (58 km/h)!

EYE SPY DRAGONFLY

GIVE IT UP FOR GRASSHOPPERS

Believe it or not there are over 20,000 different species of grasshopper and cricket! They belong to the insect family called orthoptera— "orthos" meaning "straight" and "pteron" meaning "wing." The family includes locusts, ground hoppers, and katydids.

Where did the wart-biter get its name

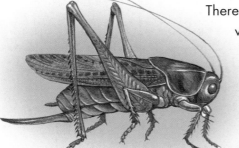

There was a time when wart-biter crickets were used to bite off warts, so you might want to think twice before picking them up!

A wart-biter cricket.

What makes a grasshopper sing

Next time you hear a grasshopper sing take it as a sign that love is in the air! Male grasshoppers sing to woo females and to warn off other males. They create their song in a variety of amazing ways. Some rub their hind legs against their forewings and some rub their wings together.

How high can a grasshopper jump ?

Grasshoppers are natural long jumpers. Your average grasshopper can jump to at least twenty times its own body length. That's the human equivalent of almost 120 ft (36.6 m).

How does a cricket hear

Next time you get close to a cricket, take a peek at its kneecaps! Just below the knee on each of its front legs there is a swelling and this swelling enables the cricket to hear what's going on. Leg-tastic!

What is a locust ?

Locusts are part of a large group of jumping insects called grasshoppers. They differ from grasshoppers, which are generally solitary, well-camouflaged insects, in that they can change their behavior. When conditions, such as temperature and rainfall, are absolutely right, they go into a breeding frenzy, producing millions of offspring. These young insects are often quite brightly colored, can migrate over long distances, and live together in millions—sometimes billions! A locust swarm can do terrible damage to a farmer's crop in a very short space of time and they are much feared in Africa and Asia.

Locusts can cause serious damage to farmers' crops.

FACT BYTES

Since Biblical times, locusts and grasshoppers have provided a tasty snack containing 50 percent protein! John the Baptist was said to have lived on locusts and honey, and today these insects still feature as a standard ingredient of Middle Eastern and Chinese cuisine. Simply remove the wings, the small legs and the head… season and serve!

GIVE IT UP FOR GRASSHOPPERS

FLUTTERBY BUTTERFLY

There are at least 150,000 different species of moth but only about 15,000 species of butterfly. They are both part of the lepidoptera group—"lepido" meaning scale and "ptera" meaning wing.

Can butterflies resist injury ?

As a rule, no—but the monarch butterfly has evolved a kind of leathery skin. Birds often peck at butterflies on their thorax which usually kills them, but the monarch's tougher skin can withstand the bird's pecking. The bird, expecting an easy meal, becomes confused and, in the confusion, the monarch flies away unharmed. An ordinary butterfly would be pecked to pieces and gobbled up, but the monarch survives.

What's the difference between butterflies and moths ?

While both creatures have four wings that are usually covered in colored scales, butterflies like to show off their beautiful colors by flying in the daytime and resting with their wings closed. Moths, however, like to fly at night and are often more muted in color. Moths have fat, furry bodies and prefer to rest with their wings open. Butterflies have little bumps at the end of their antennae while moths do not. Butterflies nearly always have less hairy bodies than moths, which are covered in little bristles. Moths have "hooks" that link their front and back wings—butterflies do not.

How does a butterfly taste its food ?

If you've watched a butterfly sitting on a leaf consider that you might be interrupting its lunch! Butterflies taste using their six feet. The female does this to make sure that the plant is the right variety for laying eggs on.

FACT BYTES

Adult butterflies do not eat— they only drink. When their feet touch a tasty liquid, they unroll their proboscis, or "feeding" tube and suck up the liquid, quenching their thirst with flower nectar or even rotting fruit juice. Aah, that's better!

What's the biggest butterfly in the world

Well, for a start she's female and she's named after a queen… the Queen Alexandra birdwing. This rare and poisonous beauty has a wingspan of up to 11 in. (28 cm) with cream markings on a chocolate-brown background and a bright yellow abdomen. Rarely seen, both the male and females fly high in the rainforest canopy of Papua, New Guinea.

The Queen Alexandra birdwing.

Which moth sounds like a bird

If you're lucky enough to come across the hummingbird hawk moth, you could be forgiven for thinking it's a bird—especially as, to confuse you further, it flies during the daytime! This expert hoverer darts from flower to flower, beating its wings as it does so until you can hear it hum. It has a wingspan of 2 in. (50-58 mm) and is often mistaken for a hummingbird.

A hummingbird hawk moth.

What's the largest moth

With a wingspan averaging around 12 in. (300 mm), the atlas moth, with its beautiful ruby-colored wings, is a truly impressive sight! It lives in the jungles of Malaysia, and uses the large white "eye spots" on its wings to warn predators off. Despite the ferocious defence camouflage, though, the atlas moth has a rather sad tale to tell. While the atlas caterpillar munches away to develop into this mammoth moth, the atlas moth itself has no stomach. This means that it cannot take in food, and only lives for around a day.

An atlas moth.

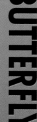

BUSY BODIES

There are over 19,000 known species of bee and a similar number of wasps —but these are only the ones we know about! Both are a gardener's friend. Bees pollinate flowers and wasps like to eat common garden pests such as caterpillars and aphids.

Why do wasps like picnics ?

On a hot summer's day the worker wasp population is at its height and because wasps love sugary foods, a picnic for you is a picnic for them, too! If you react by waving your arms and screaming at them, this unfortunately encourages them to invite their friends along—ever noticed that? What you should do is prepare a separate picnic for the wasps—a plate with some sweet, sticky jelly on or a bottle of cola put at a safe distance will do, so that they can join in without upsetting anyone.

How do bees make honey ?

Bees have two stomachs—one is specially for storing honey. Field bees suck the nectar from flowers and store it in their honey tummy. Filling the honey tummy takes between 100-1,500 flower visits. Returning to the hive, worker bees suck the nectar out and when it is regurgitated, it's spread through the honeycomb and fanned by their busy wings until it forms honey.

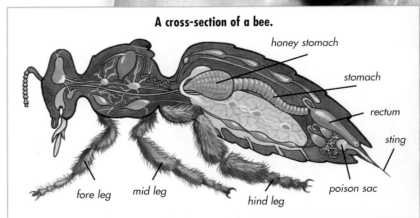

A cross-section of a bee.

honey stomach

stomach

rectum

sting

poison sac

fore leg

mid leg

hind leg

What happens to a bee when it stings ?

Bees do have a sharp sting in their tail that is reserved for warding off unsuspecting predators. Unfortunately for the bee, when it has to give in and sting something, the sting and its abdomen tears away. The bee dies as a result!

Do wasps eat spiders ?

This one does! The tarantula hawk wasp is very partial to spiders. As its name implies, the female tarantula hawk watches, waits and pounces on the tarantula before paralyzing it with her sting. She then lays an egg on it and pushes it into her burrow—the spider's burial chamber. The spider cannot rest in peace, though, because once the wasp grub has hatched, it feeds on the still living but paralyzed spider. Ouch!

The tarantula hawk wasp.

Are hornets aggressive ?

The European hornet (right) is a type of wasp and can inflict a very nasty sting. It is larger than the common wasp, but is, in fact, more docile, despite its size and ferocious appearance. However, if it is molested or feels threatened it can, and will, deliver a vicious and painful sting. Unlike bees, a wasp can sting repeatedly and will not die as a result.

What's the difference between bees and wasps ?

You may think that all bees and wasps are just buzzing, stinging, yellow and black insects, but there are ways to tell them apart. Bees have short hairs all over their bodies—even their eyes—which makes them look soft and fuzzy. Honey bees can often be seen carrying pollen back to their hive in little "baskets" on their hind legs. Bumble bees are larger and rounder, but they are still hairy. Wasps, on the other hand, have a thin "waist" and smooth, shiny bodies. Their yellow and black markings are much sharper and brighter than a bee's. Just to confuse you, though, the most colorful bees of all are the orchid bees.

FACT BYTES

The tarantula hawk wasp is also the biggest wasp in the world with a wingspan of about 5 in. (12 cm).

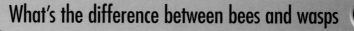

ANT-TASTIC

Ants and termites are known as "social" insects because they live in groups. The group could be as few as twenty or as big as many thousand and is called a colony. Did you know that there are more termites on Earth than human beings?

What happens inside a colony

Amazingly, there are 8,800 known species of ants in the world—and there are probably many more that we don't know about! Different ants have very different lifestyles, but the ones we know most about are those who live in colonies as worker ants. Workers are known as "neuter" ants, meaning that they are neither male nor female. They gather food, look after the young ants, defend the colony (nest) and look after the queen. During the year, the queen ant will lay some "special" eggs which grow into ants of separate sexes, both male and female. The males and females set off to mate—this is known as the "nuptial flight," as unlike their neuter family members, they have wings. Once mated, each female becomes the queen of a new colony.

What do ants eat

Driver, or army ants mass in their thousands and eat anything that is too slow to escape. They will eat rats, mice, spiders, other insects, snakes, lizards—absolutely anything. It has been recorded that a horde of African army ants ate three dead goats in three days! Not bad for a small insect! Luckily, they only live in the tropics, but should you come across some, don't be brave—run like mad!

Which termites make the tallest nest

The African termite takes the prize! Starting underground, its nest can measure up to 42 ft (12.8 m) high, emerging above the earth with umbrella-shaped layers. That's the equivalent of seven tall people standing on top of one another.

A cross-section of a termite nest.

How do ants talk to each other

Ants have two ways of communicating in order to pass on messages about the nest, their food or their enemies. They do this by creating special chemicals called pheromones that other ants can smell. If this doesn't work they take a more direct approach and use their antennae to tap their message on to the other ant!

What does a queen ant do all day

The queen ant is responsible for laying the eggs. This means that all the other ants in the colony must look after her, clean her, protect her and feed her. What a great life for the queen!

Where does the honeypot ant get its name

If you'd ever seen one you'd know why! This amazing ant lives in semi-desert regions and during the rainy season, it's fed with water and nectar until its abdomen swells up. Then, when the dry season starts and there's not much food around, it can be a useful walking larder to the other hungry ants. Dig in!

A honey pot ant.

Worker ants with the queen.

FACT BYTES

Termite damage in a house is a bigger threat than tornado, fire, lightning damage or even a hurricane! This is because termites never sleep, they do not hibernate and they like to eat wood, books, carpets, furniture, window frames, flooring... argh!

ANT-TASTIC

EAT UP

Insects have varied feeding habits and their feeding parts are designed specially to munch through the dinner of the day. Some insects can eat just about anything—others are more selective.

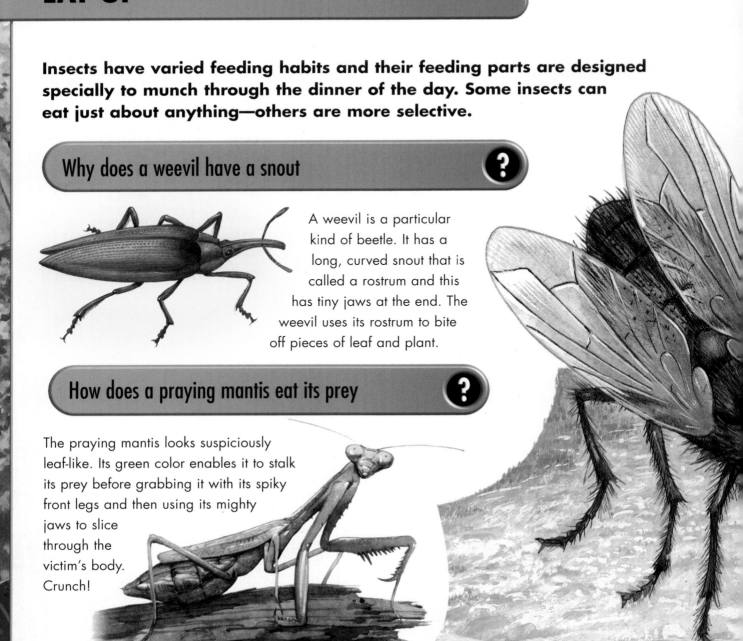

Why does a weevil have a snout ?

A weevil is a particular kind of beetle. It has a long, curved snout that is called a rostrum and this has tiny jaws at the end. The weevil uses its rostrum to bite off pieces of leaf and plant.

How does a praying mantis eat its prey ?

The praying mantis looks suspiciously leaf-like. Its green color enables it to stalk its prey before grabbing it with its spiky front legs and then using its mighty jaws to slice through the victim's body. Crunch!

How do mosquitoes spread disease ?

Blood-sucking mosquitoes drink blood and any germs that are contained within it. When the mosquito decides to feast on a new victim, it can pass on diseases that are caused by bacteria, parasites, or viruses. Before too long, this messy eater has done a marvelous job of spreading disease!

FACT BYTES

Butterflies and moths feed with a long tube called a proboscis. When they are not feeding, they pack the proboscis neatly away like a portable briefcase.

Which beetle has the most disgusting feeding habit ?

The carrion beetle has to be a strong contender for the title. This glossy, dark-colored beetle loves to munch on the decomposing flesh of dead animals. Sometimes they hide under it, other times, you may find them wandering around the insides. However, they cannot live on decomposing flesh alone and die if they do not have a healthy supply of maggots to keep them going.

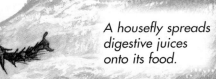
A housefly spreads digestive juices onto its food.

What are parasites ?

A parasite is any animal that lives off another, different animal without giving anything in return. The itch mite is a good example of this and can live off humans who do not wear sufficiently protective clothing. The mite burrows underneath the skin and lays eggs. The eggs emerge as larvae two or three days later. All their activity under the skin can be itchy, but, of course, scratching only makes it worse and can lead to infection.

Why are house flies sick ?

Well, they're not exactly sick but they do like to land on food and if it seems appealing they then spread digestive juices on to it—just as though they were vomiting! The food turns soft and the fly can dab at it with its sponge-like mouthparts—squelch!

What does an ant use mandibles for ?

Ants have jaws specifically designed to chop up food and these are known as mandibles. The ant uses these mandibles to bite and cut up its food, for excavation, to build nests and as a weapon.

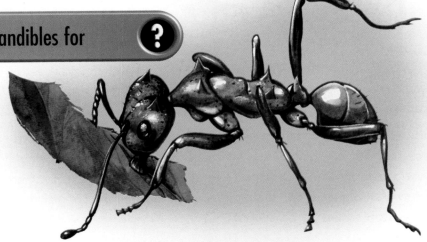

LEGGY, LEGGY, LEGGY!

You've seen creepy crawlies scuttle and crawl along floors and up walls, but have you ever stopped to wonder just how amazing their legs are? If it weren't for their amazing legs, many of these insects wouldn't be able to leap, bound, and generally get around?

Are fleas afraid of heights

Judging by the way they can jump, what do you think? Fleas are famous for jumping as high as 12 in. (30 cm), which is pretty amazing for such a tiny creature. Fleas lift off with 140 times the force of gravity.

Do centipedes have hundred legs

A millipede.

Contray to popular belief, centipedes actually have fewer than a hundred legs. They have one pair of legs on each body segment. They have specially adapted front legs with poisonous fangs on them which can give a nasty bite.

How does a desert cricket avoid getting sunstroke

Desert crickets use their legs for leaping, but more importantly, if they're caught in the heat of the midday sun, they can quickly turn their legs to another use. Guess what it is! It quickly digs itself into the sand where it can hide from the heat or from any predators. Feathery feet make it easier for the cricket to walk on sand, and their long legs lift them off the hot ground, where even a lift of 1/3 in. (5 mm) could be 86°F cooler!

How do water beetles escape predators

One type of water beetle, the camphor beetle, uses its legs to ski on the water's surface. To escape from predators, it shoots a chemical from its back legs that reduces the water surface tension. This means that the water surface tension on its front legs pulls it forwards. It zooms out of trouble on its front feet which are held out like skis, and steers itself by flexing its abdomen. This tiny beetle is the size of a rice grain, but can travel nearly three feet per second in this way! Another water beetle, the whirligig, dives into water to avoid predators, breathing from a bubble of air trapped in its rear end.

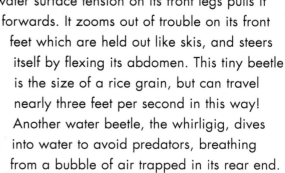

A desert cricket digging into the sand to hide from predators or cool down.

How does a locust jump

A locust ready to lift off is an impressive sight. First it keeps its back legs folded ready to jump. Then the leg muscles straighten out and launch it into the air. High in the air, the locust uses its wings to fly forward before spreading its legs wide to ensure a safe landing. Ta da!

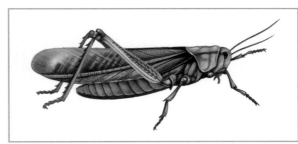

A locust ready to jump.

FACT BYTES

Giant crane flies (you may know them as daddy-long-legs) have breakaway legs that enable them to fly off if caught. Its unsuspecting predator will be left with a spindly meal of leg minus fly, and the crane fly can continue on its way with five of its six legs!

A locust using its wing to fly.

A locust beginning to land.

LEGGY, LEGGY, LEGGY!

21

STAYING ALIVE

It's a jungle out there—particularly for insects struggling to survive without being eaten by predators! Insects have developed cunning means of self-defense and some even re-grow injured legs or antennae.

Which beetle is the most scary

Stay away from a bombadier beetle! As is common in the natural world, their red coloring could be a warning signal. Danger! Stay away! When this beetle is angry or provoked, it fires a mixture of chemicals from special glands situated in their rear end. One species fires the chemicals as a constant jet (like a hose), it is possible that other types release their spray at intervals. A complicated system of chemical reactions take place inside the body of the beetle, creating such a high pressure that boiling point is reached.

What is a "toe biter"

The giant water bug has special flattened back legs to help it swim. Its front legs are used to hold on to prey while it eats it. Brown in color, they are the largest true bugs, growing up to 2³⁄₈ in. (60 mm). They're nicknamed "toe-biters" so don't go in the water barefoot! Bizarrely, not all water bugs are keen to keep the species well and thriving—there is evidence that the parents may eat their children, holding them in their legs and sucking out their insides.

Do caterpillars sting ?

Some do although you might not think it, watching a caterpillar wriggle harmlessly along a leaf. Well, look again. Those amazing hairs that cover its body are hollow and like tiny quills. In some species each hair is connected to a poison sack that the caterpillar can use as a hidden weapon. If touched, the hairs break through the skin releasing poison—nasty!

FACT BYTES

Eyespots on the wings of butterflies and moths cause enemies to think twice before pouncing. Look at the eyed hawk moth—it's pretty scary!

A male stag beetle defeats a rival.

Why do earwigs have pincers ?

These creatures need to keep their wits about them. If you're ever lucky enough to find an earwig, pick it up gently and you may find that in return you get a small nip! At the end of its abdomen, an earwig has a pair of pincers that it uses to tuck its wings away. These pincers also come in handy for staving off unwanted attention from predators.

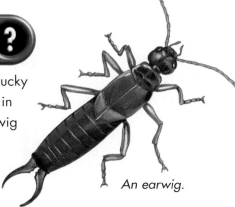

An earwig.

What is a false scorpion ?

A false scorpion looks like a scorpion but isn't. This is extremely useful in deterring predators which fear the sting of a true scorpion's tail. The false scorpion has no sting. Can you run backward as fast as you can run forward? The false scorpion can, which is another clever way to avoid being eaten!

How do stag beetles fight each other ?

If a male stag beetle meets another male stag beetle, he stretches out his antennae to detect vital information. He then tries to look as threatening as he can. If that doesn't work, he'll resort to using his antler-like jaws to wrestle his rival to the ground. If he's lucky, his jaws will puncture the loser's tough armor and leave him dying on his back.

Why are moth wings dusty ?

If you've ever touched a moth you've probably found your fingertips covered in what looks like dust. In fact, butterfly and moth wings are made up of tiny scales. This is to protect them from predators. If they fly into a spider's web, the scales fall off easily and they can flutter off and escape— cunning, eh?

Insects are masters of the art of camouflage. They can mimic other creatures and plants in order to pass unnoticed, or they can simply hide away, disguised as the object they are hiding on. The clue is very often in the name...

What is a katydid ?

Katydids, with their long antennae and shiny bodies, are crazy looking insects that get their name from the song of the "true" katydid, the longhorned grasshopper that sings a song that goes "ka-ty-did, ka-ty-did-n't." They have existed for over 300 million years, and their truly amazing capacity for camouflage must be a strong reason for this. You are unlikely to see one, as their glossy green bodies blend in with their leafy surroundings, safe from any passing bird as they munch away.

When is a leaf not a leaf ?

When it's a leaf butterfly! This amazing butterfly looks just like a leaf. Apart from its brown leafy color, it has leaf ribs, fungus spots and even a leaf stalk—you'd have to have excellent eyesight to spot it lurking!

A leaf butterfly.

Where does the walking stick get its name ?

Just one look at the amazing "walking stick" stick insect with its slow body movements, long body shape and brown color is enough to prove where its name comes from. Looking at these insects on a tree you'd find it very hard to see them as they look just like twigs to you and me.

FACT BYTES

To avoid being mistaken for a tasty snack, some caterpillars disguise themselves as leaves. Birds are especially partial to caterpillars and this is why some clever caterpillars pretend to be bird droppings. Well, who can blame them?

Which Malaysian flower is also an insect

The beautiful Malaysian orchid mantis has pointed eyes, petal-like shapes on its legs and is colored a pretty pale pink—just like the flower. Not only is this a clever camouflage but it also leads unsuspecting pollinating insects to come in for a drink thinking it's a flower. What happens next? Capture and a certain meal for the mantis!

Malaysian orchid mantis.

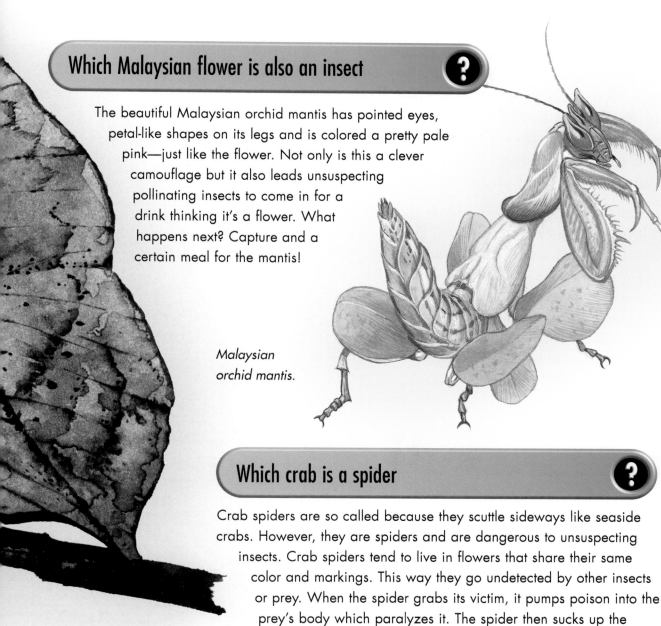

Which crab is a spider

Crab spiders are so called because they scuttle sideways like seaside crabs. However, they are spiders and are dangerous to unsuspecting insects. Crab spiders tend to live in flowers that share their same color and markings. This way they go undetected by other insects or prey. When the spider grabs its victim, it pumps poison into the prey's body which paralyzes it. The spider then sucks up the victim's body fluids—yum, yum!

Which fly pretends it's a wasp

The cleverly disguised hover fly bears the same coloring and pattern as a wasp—an effective way of warding off predators. Unlike wasps, it won't bite or sting you so all you need do is remember which is which! The simplest way is to watch it fly. Hover flies are named after their hovering flight.

A hover fly.

UP, UP, AND AWAY!

The way in which insects have managed to survive for million of years is largely thanks to the fact that they can fly. Without wings they would find it much harder to escape from danger, to find food or to look for a new place to live. Imagine how easy it would be to move house if all you needed to do was flap your wings and head skyward.

Can insects fly backward **?**

Yes, some insects can! Dragonflies can hover like helicopters, fly vertically, they can stop or suddenly change direction in mid-flight… oh, and they can also fly backward. The fastest flier was probably a giant prehistoric dragonfly. It was so large that it had to fly as fast as 43 mph (69 km/h) to stop it from crashing.

Can insects travel long distance **?**

Yes they can! Some insects have special wings that can help them glide for long distances. One of these is the African grasshopper— check out its broad hind wings, which are perfect for the job.

Giant prehistoric dragonflies.

An African grasshopper.

Insects have such thin wings, why

Insect wings are thin and light so they don't weigh them down. They have to beat their wings fast in order to warm up their flight muscles so that the wings can get moving. A bit like the way humans do warm-up exercises before sport!

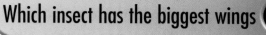

Which insect has the biggest wings ❓

The hercules moth from Australia has an amazing wingspan of 11 in. (28 cm)—that's bigger than any other insect! If you see this one coming, for goodness' sake turn off the light!

Australian hercules moth.

Can spiders fly ❓

Well, no, they can't—but they can and do travel vast distances in the air. Small spiders, or young ones which are called spiderlings, can be blown along by the wind across land and sea and this may explain why spiders are found on islands. Some spiderlings have been caught in remotely operated weather stations thousands of feet up in the sky!

FACT BYTES

Bees beat their wings as fast as 180 beats per second—phew!

Why do moths fly at the light ❓

Have some sympathy for the moth next time you see one go flying into a light bulb or candle flame. It's probably a bit confused by the artificial light. Some experts think that moths navigate by moonlight which is why they seem to be literally blinded by the light in our living rooms.

Moths flying towards the moon.

UP, UP, AND AWAY!

LET'S GET TOGETHER

Most female insects must find a mate of their own kind in order to lay eggs. Contrary to what you might think, there are many different rituals of insect courtship and some of them are quite similar to humans!

Do insects make love signals ?

A firefly.

Male fireflies flash their lights at female fireflies in order to attract a mate. Females are attracted to the male whose light lasts longest. This is because she reads this as a signal that he will make a good father. The male has to make sure that she's of the same species before he lands—otherwise he'll discover that he's the main course on the menu for her dinner date. Not a very nice end to a romantic evening!

Is mating dangerous ?

It is to a male praying mantis—the female sees him as just another meal! The male must stealthily creep up on the female and then jump on her to mate. Should they be disturbed, she will kill and eat him—head first! Bad news for the male, but the female's eggs are fertilized and she enjoys a thoroughly good meal!

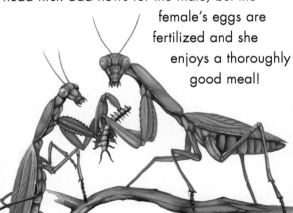

Do insects give presents ?

Some insects feed on other insects—this can be tricky for an amorous male. To stop himself from being eaten up when they mate, he first presents the female with a special edible love token of another dead insect.

Dancing
butterflies.

Why does scent matter

The insect world is full of chemical signals called pheromones. Moths have sensitive feather-like antennae that they use to detect long-distance love signals from a mate. Moon moths in India can smell the scent from over 6¼ miles (11 km) away. The female emperor moth only comes out at night so she leaves a strong perfume wafting in the air to help the male to find her.

Which insect sings love songs

Next time you hear a grasshopper chirping it may mean that love is in the air. It rubs its back legs along its front wing so that it can serenade females of the species.

Do insects like to dance ?

Yes they do! Butterflies perform special dancing flights to make sure they have found the perfect mate from the right species. Dancing helps to exchange the pheromones that will tell them they have found the right partner. Male scorpions are more brazen—they actually take hold of the female and lead her into a courtship dance!

FACT BYTES

With only one day to live, mate and lay eggs, the aquatic insect called the mayfly gets the reward for being the fastest romancer of the bug world.

DEADLY CLOTHES

Some of the world's deadliest and most dangerous creatures belong to the insect world. Can you guess what they are?

Is this a snake ?

No—it is, in fact, a caterpillar, but it looks just like a small snake which might have a deadly, venomous bite. It is a hawkmoth caterpillar which, when alarmed or disturbed, raises its head and inflates its thorax with air to mimic a snake. It even has false "snake eyes" for good effect. Deadly clothes—yes—but completely harmless!

A hawkmoth caterpillar.

A swarm of African honeybees.

Does a black widow deserve its reputation ?

The black widow is one of the world's most infamous deadly spiders. It inhabits the warmer regions of the world and is especially common in eastern and central parts of the US. The venomous female black widow is shiny black, usually with a reddish hourglass shape on the underside of her body. Adult males, on the other hand, are harmless. The black widow's venom is fifteen times as toxic as that of a rattlesnake but because she does not inject much poison human fatalities are thankfully rare. Like most spiders, the black widow preys on insects. After ensnaring her prey in a web, the black widow makes small punctures in the victim's body and sucks out the liquid contents. The female black widow may have a reputation for killing and eating its male partner but this is the exception rather than the rule.

Which insect spreads a "sleeping sickness" ?

The tsetse fly found in Africa likes to feed on animal and human blood. Since way back in the fourteenth century, Africans have been battling with this insect and the fatal "sleeping sickness" disease it spreads. One bite can transmit a parasite that works its way through the body and if left untreated, the victim will die a slow and painful death.

A tsetse fly.

Do killer bees really exist ?

African honeybees or "killer" bees are a very real threat. In the USA they remain a dangerous and deadly enemy. They are so-called because they are easily annoyed and once they're angry, they stay that way—sometimes taking it out on their victims for an entire day! Worse still, they target the head and face and if you think jumping into water will help, think again! Killer bees will wait for you to come up for air then sting you again.

FACT BYTES

The South American fire ant is responsible for biting over 25,000 people in the US per year! Once bitten, you will suffer a fiery sting that becomes a blister. Fire ants are very aggressive so it's probably best to steer clear.

What is Africa's deadliest insect ?

The mosquito! It alone is responsible for the deaths of more people in Africa than any other creature. It carries malaria and other tropical diseases, which it passes on when it bites.

Can an ant sting ?

The giant tropical bullet ant delivers a nasty sting that gives it its name. Victims have described the severe sting as feeling like a bullet and the pain lasts for 3-5 hours. Worker bullet ants can be as big as 1 in. (18-25 mm) long so at least you can see them coming.

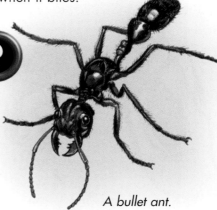

A bullet ant.

RAINFOREST RARITIES

The biggest rainforest covers an area of 2.7 million sq miles (7 million sq km) around the Amazon River in South America. The climate is perfect for animals, plants and insects because it is always hot and it rains every day.

A monarch butterfly.

Which butterfly leaves an after-taste ?

The brightly colored orange monarch butterfly looks tempting to predators but if eaten the predator will soon regret it. The monarch's poison doesn't kill but it makes the predator sick—something the predator remembers next time it's passing.

How do rainforest natives use ants ?

Army ants have such large jaws that they can enlarge them to bite animals harder. Rainforest natives soon came to notice this and decided the army ants could help them. Squeezing the ant from behind, the ant would bite down on a wound and this would make a handy stitch to prevent infection!

An army ant.

Rainforests are home to many colorful insects.

Which rainforest insect tucks itself into bed at night ?

The morpho butterfly has brilliant blue wings that make it stand out as one of the most beautiful butterflies in the world. In order to ensure sweet dreams and no nightmare predator attacks, the morpho tucks away its brightly colored wings so that it can blend into the environment. It hangs from trees or the underside of leaves.

A morpho butterfly.

Which insect keeps the food chain going ?

The mainly carnivorous praying mantis can fade into the background and lie in wait for its prey. It is vital to the food chain because it eats all kinds of different insects.

Which ants help to maintain the enviroment ?

Leaf-cutter ants carry leaves down to their colonies where they chew them into fungus—their favorite food! The by-products of this process adds fertilizer to the topsoil of the rainforest.

Leaf-cutter ants at work.

FACT BYTES

A single colony of army ants can amount to as many as 700,000 ants living off the forest floor. Army ants will have a bite of anything that crosses their path.

RAINFOREST RARITIES

WATER BABIES

Take a closer look next time you're at the riverbank—it's a haven for a whole world of water insects. Most insects breathe through the holes in the sides of their bodies and would suffocate without any air. Water or "aquatic" insects are specially adapted to living in water so that they can't drown.

What's so special about whirligigs

The whirligig is the only water beetle that can swim on the water's surface. It uses its legs like paddles to row its way across the pond or lake and can be seen scurrying about the pond's surface in large numbers.

What is a water tiger

This is a beetle! It is called a water tiger, because it is so ferocious and has an enormous appetite. It has even been known to bite the fingers of insect collectors! Water tigers have extremely powerful jaws which they use to great effect when disemboweling tadpoles or penetrating the flesh of beetles before devouring them!

What do giant water bugs eat

The clue is in the name! The giant water bug or "fish killer" is one of the largest aquatic insects and makes a scary underwater predator. It likes to eat small fish, frogs, snails and tadpoles. It can be as big as 3 in. (7 cm) long and breathes through its tail that is specially modified to act like a snorkel.

Which water insect can walk on water ❓

The aptly named pond skater or water strider has a long, narrow body and six spidery legs. It stays afloat thanks to special water-repellent hairs that cover its underside. If you're lucky enough to see one you can watch how it uses its hind legs as rudders and its middle legs to propel itself across the surface of the water. Its short forelegs are to help it catch prey.

A pond skater.

FACT BYTES

Whirligigs are also known as "apple smellers" because they smell fruity when they are picked up!

A dragonfly nymph.

Which water insect lives at the bottom of the pond ❓

It's the dragonfly nymph (think of it as a teenage dragonfly) and measures anything between $^2/_3$ in.–2 in. (18-49 mm) long. This clever insect doesn't need to come up for air because it can breathe by sucking water in, absorbing the oxygen and then squeezing the water out again to jet propel itself through the water.

GOING UNDERGROUND

Insects have been living on Earth for so long that they have had plenty of time to adapt to living almost anywhere on, above or underneath the ground. Next time you're out in the garden think about what tiny creatures might be living right underneath you!

Do insects need to come up for air ?

Having their skeletons on the outside of their bodies, insects breathe in a different way to you and me. Spiracles are tiny holes along the sides of their body that act like tiny portholes enabling the insect to breathe passively, whether they are above or below the ground.

spiracles

Is this a mole ?

Mole crickets do have a passing resemblance to moles for a very good reason. Their powerful, flattened front legs are very good shovels allowing the cricket to burrow underground, where they eat roots and vegetation with specially adapted shear-like mouthparts.

Which insect helps to turn over the soil ?

There are at least 2,700 different kinds of these amazing wriggling creatures! Have you guessed yet? Earthworms! Tunneling deep into the soil, earthworms turn the soil over and over like a plough. This creates tunnels that aerate the soil so that water can penetrate and all the time, the topsoil and the sub soil are mixed together. This makes earthworms nature's help to gardeners.

An earthworm.

Which singing insect can live underground for 17 years

Believe it or not some species of cicada can! Cicadas belong to the hemiptera family, which means like bugs and aphids; they have piercing, sucking mouthparts. Cicada nymphs (not yet grown-up) live underground on a feast of plant sap—some for as long as 13 or 17 years! When it has reached full-size, the cicada uses its special front legs to dig its way up to the surface before climbing on to a tree trunk and shedding its skin.

Which insects party

The hard-working ants of course! Ants are masters of the art of creating underground nests that are designed for maximum comfort and efficiency. Worker ants dig tunnels to make hallways connecting the chambers. The queen ant has one large chamber of her own in which she can keep her eggs. Nurseries are built so that workers can look after the brood, and once they start growing up, family rooms are waiting where the colony can party!

FACT BYTES

During summer, ants get busy storing food in specially designed underground larders.

In the winter they help themselves to their special food stores.

Why is it so hard to pull a worm out of the ground

You may have watched a hungry blackbird busy tugging at the soil and it's a safe bet that there's a tug-of-war going on between the worm and the bird. Well, who can blame the worm for putting up a fight? The worm has four pairs of hooks called setae that can stick to soil particles and conveniently make it very hard to budge!

GOING UNDERGROUND

DESERT BUGS

You might expect the dry and barren landscape of the desert to be too hot for insects to survive. The heat alone you'd think would kill them! However, a bug's eye view will soon reveal just how many of these amazing creatures have adapted to life under the sun.

Which desert bugs rarely drink ?

Scorpions and camel spiders! Both are specially adapted to their arid environment and have a very low rate of water loss, taking all the liquid they need from their victims. Sensibly, they are nearly all nocturnal, spending their days shaded in burrows or under rocks preserving their energy to hunt by night.

Which insect is deadly to crops ?

The desert locust! When young, the swarming species of desert locust form groups of around 20,000 and hop about on the sand looking for food. As they grow up and learn to fly they become even more dangerous. Swarms of locusts will fly over the desert eating everything in their path and traveling up to 400 sq miles (1,036 sq km) per day. There could be as many as 40 billion insects swarming, capable of destroying 40,000 tonnes of plants in one day!

How else do insects get water to drink ?

The darkling beetle, which lives in the extremely dry Namib Desert of Africa, gets moisture in a very clever way. Early each morning, it sets off up to the shady side of a dune, where it stands with its head pointing down the slope and its rear up in the air. As the morning mist clears, some of its moisture collects on the ridged back of the beetle until a drop forms. This drop then gently rolls down the length of the beetle towards its mouth, and it can take a drink!

A darkling beetle.

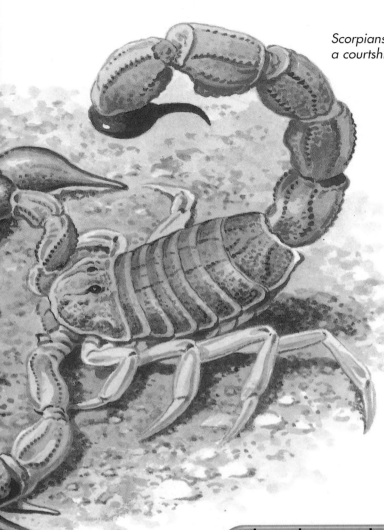

Scorpians performing a courtship dance.

A camel spider.

When is a camel not a camal ?

When it's a great big camel spider! This mighty cross between a spider and a scorpion can be as big as 6 in. (15 cm) long and can run like the wind up to speeds of 10 mph (16 km/h). That might explain its other name of "wind scorpion." Like scorpions, camel spiders hunt at night. They prey on scorpions, lizards, mice, and even birds!

Why is the giant desert scorpion covered in hair ?

Living in the desert regions of California and Arizona, this hairy monster's body is covered in brown hairs to help it detect air and ground vibrations. Lurking under rocks in the heat of the day, its body can be as big as a camel spider awarding it the prize for biggest scorpion in North America.

A giant desert scorpion.

FACT BYTES

Scorpions and spiders are part of the arachnid family. The Sahara scorpion lives on insects and spiders. It seizes its prey with its pincers before injecting a lethal poison from its tail. Its sting is potent enough to kill an adult human being!

SWAMP MONSTERS

Swamp habitats provide an excellent environment for aquatic insects such as dragonflies and mosquitoes. Either completely or partially wooded with trees and shrubs, a swamp is, in fact, teeming with animal, plant, and insect life.

What are midges ❓

Midges are small flies that fly around in large swarms near and around water. The larvae perform an extremely useful task as they feed on bacteria and are very important in the disposal of human waste in sewage plants. They may not look like much, but they help to keep our environment clean and healthy.

Which everglade insect weaves golden silk ❓

The golden orb weaver spider! This beautiful yellow, black and white spider spins silk webs that have a golden sheen to them high in the hammocks of the everglades. The webs are semi-permanent, trapping insects, bats and even small birds. The spider cleans the web every day to make sure that its trap is kept free from leaf debris and twigs that would give the game away to unsuspecting victims.

A golden orb weaver spider.

Which swamp insect has survived from ancient times ❓

The giant dragonfly! This rare survivor of ancient times can be (rarely) spotted in New South Wales. Its brown and yellow body can be as thick as a human finger and nine species of this fantastic creature are thought to be still alive—but only just.

A giant dragonfly.

Which beautiful beetle has been made into jewelry ?

The metallic wood-boring beetle from Ecuador has amazing iridescent wing cases and they reflect nearly every color of the rainbow! The Shaur tribes of the Amazon use this beautiful creature to make decorative ornaments that they believe symbolize wealth and power. Luckily this large beetle is good at flying so it can try to escape!

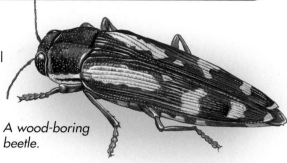

A wood-boring beetle.

Why do earwigs have pincers ?

At caterpillar stage, the bagworm moth produces bags that can be up to 2 in. (5 cm) long and ⅜ in. (1.3 cm) wide. These bags are made from silk with fragments of leaves, twigs, bark and sometimes even snail shells woven into them. The caterpillars retreat inside the bags, which are visible in the trees.

The three lifestages of the bagworm moth.

Swamps provide excellent homes for many aquatic insects.

FACT BYTES

Mosquitoes thrive in swamps. They like to live in dark wet areas, close to water where they can lay their eggs and where there are plenty of plants for them to suck dry.

HOUSE OF HORRORS

So far you may think that most of the insects you've read about are simply too far away to worry about... well don't forget that some insects are just as happy living in your home as you are!

What is a woodworm ?

Woodworm are the larvae of beetles that grow up to be wood-gnawers. Unfortunately, even at this undeveloped, grub-like stage, these larvae have a taste for pine, oak, you name it. In the open, they like to eat chunks out of trees, and in the home, can be found hollowing out table legs and timbers. Examples of woodworm are the furniture beetle and the deathwatch beetle, who'll appear when the wood is attacked by fungal decay.

How do spiders help humans ?

Spiders are very useful for humans. By controlling the population of pests, such as aphids, spiders reduce the damage to commercial crops and protect people from disease bearing insects. However, many spiders are killed by insecticides and destruction of their natural environments.

What is a woodlouse ?

Woodlice may look like insects, but in fact they are crustaceans and are related to sea creatures, like crabs and lobsters. There are over 3,000 species of woodlice in the world with around 35-40 of these being found in the UK. Woodlice love damp, dark places and can be found lurking under stones, old logs and in garden compost heaps. They will also turn up in the cold, dark corners of your house! They have fourteen legs and a segmented outer shell called an exoskeleton.

Which beetle feeds on oak ?

The deathwatch! Its alarming name comes from the legend that an ill person might hear the deathwatch tapping and, if so, death was said to be imminent. Charming! Nowadays, the threat of the deathwatch is to the oak trees it likes to munch on. Its constant chomping can weaken oak-timbered houses.

Which insect likes to eat paper ?

Primitive, nocturnal and carrot-shaped, the silverfish is only $^1/_2$–$^2/_3$ in. (15-20 mm) long. It's a pest in your house because it's especially partial to books, wallpaper… even the glue that binds your books together—It will happily munch through any or all of these! Amazingly, the silver fish is more than 400 million years old so was in existence even before dinosaurs!

Which insect likes to play sardines ?

Cockroaches of course! Living almost anywhere and prepared to eat almost anything, cockroaches can become household pests and will be pleased to share crumbs from your table with you. They have flattened bodies so are easily able to squeeze into corners and cracks where they can skulk unnoticed.

Can head lice fly ?

The good news is that they can't—they only crawl! About the size of a sesame seed, these tiny crawlers like to live in clean human hair. They hang on tight and puncture the skin with their mouthparts before sucking up some blood. Yuk!

FACT BYTES

At the end of the summer you might be lucky enough to spy a wasp nest high under the eaves of the roof. All summer long, the wasps will have been busy making their nest bigger and bigger. If you see one, leave it alone! The wasps will die naturally and if you try to move them they won't appreciate being disturbed. You have been warned!

THE EYES HAVE IT

To make up for their size, insects have highly developed senses that mean they can see and hear things that we can't. If you are able to look at an insect under the microscope, look into its eyes—they really are incredible!

What is a "compound" eye ?

Insects have two types of eyes. "Simple" eyes simply help the insect tell the difference between light and dark. "Compound" eyes are made up of thousands of lenses, and scientists believe that insects see things in a "mosaic" kind of picture. Although these eyes, unlike those of humans, are fixed in one place, the lenses allow insects to get a great picture of what's around them and can detect the slightest movement very easily.

What kind of eyes does a wasp have ?

Like many insects, wasps have simple eyes and compound eyes. It has two compound eyes and three simple eyes so now you know why it comes buzzing straight at you! Wasps, when leaving an area to which they wish to return, act as if they were locating the place, and fly about examining the area before leaving. When they return they are able to find the same exact spot, unless, meanwhile, some landmark has been removed.

How does a caterpillar see its food ?

Caterpillars live amongst their food and don't need to look far to find the next tasty leaf! They have simple eyes which means their eyesight is not very sharp—just strong enough to make out light and shade.

A caterpillar.

Wasps have both compound and single eyes.

Which insect has the best eyesight

Scientists think that insects are very short-sighted, as their eyes cannot move in their sockets and focus. Butterflies probably have the "longest" sight (of around six feet) —a bee can only see up to 20 in. (50 cm) away! But in terms of the ability to detect exactly what's around them, the eyes of a dragonfly are perhaps the most impressive. Each of its two compound eyes is made from 30,000 lenses, which allow them to catch their prey mid-flight. The dragonfly rarely stays still, darting around for food, looking left, right, up, down… all at once.

A dragonfly.

What can this fleshfly see

Nobody really knows what fleshflies see, but we do know that each compound eye comprises hundreds of single eye facets which are red in color. The fleshfly can see even the slightest movement which makes it extremely difficult for predators to catch and eat it.

Can insects see things we can't

Yes they can! Many insects are lucky enough to see ultraviolet light—the invisible light from the sun that humans and animals cannot see. This helps some pollinating insects to find their way into flowers because some flowers have petals that are lined with ultraviolet light. These lines act like runways directing the hungry insect straight into its supper!

FACT BYTES

Young butterflies begin life with simple eyes. As they reach maturity the simple eyes expand, grow and gradually become compound eyes. Compound eyes are excellent at detecting motion.

THE EYES HAVE IT

GLOSSARY

Abdomen
The rear part of the body behind the thorax.

Amber
The hard fossilized resin of extinct trees.

Antennae
A pair of mobile appendages on the heads of insects that often respond to touch and taste but may be specialized for swimming.

Aquatic insect
Lives in, or near, water.

Arachnid
A group of insects including spiders, scorpions, mites, and ticks.

Arthropod
Animals lacking a backbone, such as insects, spiders, and crustaceans.

Bacteria
A large group of typically single cell microorganisms, many of which cause disease.

Camouflage
The means by which animals escape the notice of predators.

Cannibal
An animal that feeds on the flesh of others of its kind.

Carnivorous
Feeds on other animals.

Cephalothorax
A combined head and thorax.

Chrysalis
The pupa of a moth or a butterfly, in a case or cocoon.

Colony
A community of insects living together.

Compound eye
Insect eye consisting of numerous small visual units.

Diapause
A process that makes insects inactive in cold climates.

Digestion
The act or process in living organisms of breaking down food into easily absorbed substances by the action of enzymes.

Disease
Generally an illness or sickness where normal physiological funcion is impaired.

Egg
The oval or round reproductive body laid by the females of birds, reptiles, fishes, insects, and some other animals.

Exoskeleton
A rigid external skeleton.

Fossilize
To convert or be converted into a fossil.

Glycerol
A chemical produced by insects to act as antifreeze.

Hemiptera
A large order of insects that have piercing, sucking mouthparts.

Hibernate
To pass the winter in a dormant condition with metabolism greatly slowed down.

Honeycomb
A waxy structure, constructed by bees in a hive, that consists of hexagonal cells in which honey is stored, eggs are laid, and larvae develop.

Insect
Any of a class of small air-breathing arthropods having a body divided into head, thorax, and abdomen, three pairs of legs, and (in most species) two pairs of wings.

Iridescent
Showing luminous colors that change from different angles.

Katydid
A green long-horned grasshopper living in the foliage trees of North America.

Larva
An immature free-living form of many animals that develops into a different adult form by metamorphosis.

Lepidoptera
The scale-winged insect family of moths and butterflies.

Mandibles
Jaws of an ant.

Metamorphosis
The rapid transformaion of a larva into an adult that occurs in certain animals, for example the stage between chrysalis and butterfly.

Middle Ages
The period from about 1000 AD to the 15th century.

Moulting
The process of a growing insect shedding its skin.

Navigate
To direct or plot a path.

Nectar
A sugary liquid secreted in flowers.

Nocturnal
Active at night.

Odonata
The predatory insect family of dragon and damselflies.

Ommatidia
The sections that make up a compound eye.

Orthoptera
Long-legged insect family of grasshoppers and crickets.

Paralyze
To cause a part of the body to be insensitive to pain and touch, or to make immobile.

Parasite
An animal or a plant that lives in or on another (the host) from which it obtains nourishment.

Pheromones
Chemicals produced by insects to affect the behavior of others in the same species.

Poison
Any substance that can impare function or otherwise injure the body.

Pollinate
To move pollen for fertilization.

Population
A group of individuals of the same species inhabiting a given area.

Predator
Any carnivorous animal.

Prehistoric
Of, or relating to, a man's development before the written word.

Prey
An animal hunted or captured by another for food.

Primitive
Of, relating to, or resembling an early stage in development.

Proboscis
Sucking mouth tube of moths and butterflies.

Pupa
An insect at the immobile non-feeding stage of development between larva and adult, where many internal changes occur.

Regurgitate
To vomit forth partially digested food.

Rostrum
The long, curved snout of a weevil.

Setae
Stiff bristles on a worm.

Simple eye
The small eye of an insect.

Social
Living, or preferring to live, in a community rather than alone.

Spiracle
An external breathing hole of an insect.

Swarm
A large mass of small animals, especially insects.

Thorax
The part of an insect's body between the head and the abdomen.

Virus
Any of a group of submicroscopic entities capable of replication only within the cells of animals and plants.

Wingspan
The maximum extent of the wings measured from tip to tip.

GLOSSARY

INDEX

African killer bees 31
African stick insects 2
African termites 16
Amber 1
Ants 16-17, 19, 31, 32-33, 37
Arachnids 2, 39
Army ants 16, 32-33
Assassin bugs 4

Bagworm moths 41
Bed bugs 4
Bees 14-15, 27, 31
Beetles 6-7, 21, 23, 34-35, 41, 43
Bullet ants 31
Butterflies 12-13, 23-24, 29, 32-33, 45

Camel spiders 39
Caterpillars 22, 22, 44
Cephalothorax 2
Cicadas 37
Cockroaches 43
Compound eyes 44-45
Crickets 10-11, 20

Daddy long-legs 2
Darkling beetles 38

Deathwatch beetles 42
Desert crickets 20
Desert locusts 38
Devil's coach horses 6
Diapause 3
Dragonflies 8-9, 26, 35, 40
Dung beetles 6

Earthworms 36-37
Earwigs 23
Emperor moths 29
Exoskeletons 2

Fleas 20
Fire ants 31
Fireflies 28
Flies 19, 21, 25, 31

Giant crane flies 21
Giant desert scorpion 39
Giant dragonflies 40
Giant water bugs 5, 34
Glycerol 3
Golden orb weaver spiders 40
Goliath beetles 7
Grasshoppers 10-11, 26, 29

Head lice 43
Hemiptera 4-5
Hercules moths 27
Honeypot ants 17
Hornets 15
Houseflies 19
Hover flies 25
Hummingbird hawk moths 13

Leaf butterflies 24
Lepidoptera 12-13
Locusts 10-11, 21, 38

Malaysian orchid mantis 25
Mandibles 19
Mayflies 29
Metallic wood-boring beetles 41
Millipedes 20
Moon moths 29
Monarch butterflies 32
Morpho butterflies 33
Mosquitos 9, 18, 41
Moths 12-13, 23, 27-29, 41

Odonata 8
Ommatidia 44
Orthoptera 10-11

Pheromones 17, 29
Pond skaters 35
Praying mantis 18, 33
Proboscis 5, 12, 18

Queen Alexandra birdwing butterflies 13

Scarab beetles 6, 7
Scorpions 38-39
Silverfish 43
Simple eyes 44
Spiders 2, 15, 25, 27, 38-39, 40, 42
Spiracles 36
Stag beetles 7, 23
Stick insects 2, 24
Stinkbugs 4

Tarantula hawk wasps 15
Termites 16-17
Tsetse flies 31

Walking sticks 24
Wasps 14-15, 43, 45
Wart-biter crickets 10
Weevils 18
Whirligig beetles 34-35
Woodlice 42

Acknowledgements

Key: Top - t; middle - m; bottom - b; left - l; right - r. SPL-Science Photo Library. NPL- Nature PL.

2: Sinclair Stammers/SPL. 3: Martin Gabriel/NPL. 4: John Downer/NPL. 5: James Carmichael/NHPA. 6: Andrew Parkinson/NPL. 9: (t) Corel;(b) Bernard Castelein/NPL. 10-11: Corel. 14-15: Sinclair Stammer/SPL. 17: (t) Sinclair Stammer/SPL;(b) Pascal Goetghluck/SPL. 18: Pete Billingsley/SPL. 20: Biophtos. 22: Corel. 25: Laurie Campbell/NHPA. 27: Photospin. 28: Dietmar Nill/NPL. 29: Geoff Dore/NPL.32-33: Corel. 36: Robert Thompson/NHPA. 38: Anthony Bannister/NHPA. 45: Duncan McEwan/NPL.